Songs of the CIVIL WAR

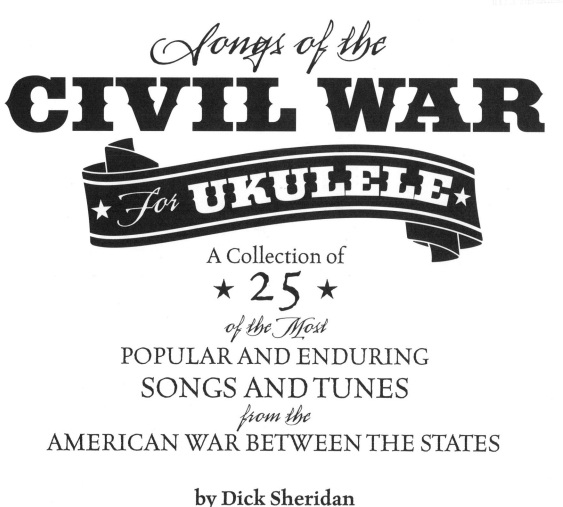

for UKULELE

A Collection of

★ 25 ★

of the Most

POPULAR AND ENDURING SONGS AND TUNES

from the

AMERICAN WAR BETWEEN THE STATES

by Dick Sheridan

ISBN 978-1-57424-277-5
SAN 683-8022

Cover by James Creative Group

CENTERSTREAM®

Copyright © 2011 CENTERSTREAM Publishing, LLC
P.O. Box 17878 - Anaheim Hills, CA 92817

www.centerstream-usa.com

"Fourscore and seven years ago our fathers brought forth upon this continent a new nation, conceived in Liberty, and dedicated to the proposition that all men are created equal. Now we are engaged in a great civil war, testing whether that nation, or any nation so conceived and so dedicated, can long endure. We are met on a great battle-field of that war. We have come to dedicate a portion of that field, as the final resting place of those who here gave their lives that that nation might live. It is altogether fitting and proper that we should do this. But, in a larger sense, we cannot dedicate, we cannot consecrate, we cannot hallow this ground. The brave men, living and dead, who struggled here, have consecrated it, far above our poor power to add or detract. The world will little note, nor long remember, what we say here, but it can never forget what they did here. It is for us, the living, rather, to be dedicated here to the unfinished work that they who fought here have thus far so nobly advanced. It is rather for us to be here dedicated to the great task remaining before us, that from these honored dead we take increased devotion to that cause for which they here gave the last full measure of devotion; that we here highly resolve that these dead shall not have died in vain; that this nation, under God, shall have a new birth of freedom, and that government of the people, by the people, for the people, shall not perish from the earth."

President Abraham Lincoln, *at the dedication of the cemetery at Gettysburg, Pennsylvania, November 19, 1863*

Table *of* Contents

From the North ... "The Union forever, hurrah! boys, hurrah!"

To the South ... "Hurrah! Hurrah! for Southern Rights, Hurrah!"

About the Author

Dick Sheridan began playing the ukulele in his grade school years when a small soprano uke and song book were given to him as a Christmas present. Daunting at first, the challenges were gradually resolved of tuning, transferring written notes to the fingerboard, and deciphering the dots and grids of chord diagrams. Along with the uke came a youngster's urge to acquire related supplies – wax paper packets of gut strings, green felt picks, pitch pipes, method books, and popular sheet music with new chord symbols and diagrams, and a host of unfamiliar tunings.

In high school, Dick learned to play the baritone uke and guitar, and then in college a tenor banjo was added to the collection during the campus revival of traditional jazz. Next came a 5-string banjo with the folk music boom of the 60s and 70s. In time, Dick went on to privately teach all of these instruments and to lead and play banjo with a Dixieland jazz band for over 40 years. Throughout, his affection for the ukulele has remained undiminished.

Dick Sheridan's interest in the Civil War period and its music developed after learning that his grandfather as a child had seen Abraham Lincoln when "Honest Abe" was on the presidential campaign trail. After Lincoln assumed office and the war started, few families were un-affected, and Dick's family was no exception. His grandfather's uncle was a surgeon with the 117th Regiment of NY Volunteers (Fourth Oneida), who later wrote and published a history of that regiment. Dick's maternal great grandfather, a minister from the upper Hudson River region, was a dedicated advocate for the pension rights of NY veterans. And even if in name only, there was the association with the Union cavalry general "Little Phil" Sheridan.

Songs *and* Tunes *of the* Civil War

From the plantations of the deep South to the rich farmlands of the Shenandoah Valley; from Atlanta by the sea to the rural cottages of the backwoods North; from slave quarters to genteel salons; from home fires to campfires; from northern Virginia to southern Pennsylvania; from Fredericksburg and Gettysburg to Washington and Richmond …

These were the tunes played on parlor spinets, by military fifes and drums, on primitive gourd banjos and hand-whittle whistles. These were the songs sung by divas and politicians, by abolitionists and secessionists, by officers on horseback and foot soldiers as they tread muddy roads in the heat of summer and the cold slush of winter …

These were the songs and tunes which boosted morale, championed causes, pulled on the heartstrings, or gave impetus to battle …

This was the music of regimental bands during the long marches, music that floated on the air in the restful times of evening encampments, melodies and words that gave spirit and courage above the thundering cacophony of canon fire and muskets …

These were the songs sung by worried mothers and lonesome sweethearts, by homesick troops in tents or trenches, by mounted cavalry or generals passing the bottle, by riflemen cleaning their weapons, by soldiers at rest playing cards or rolling dice …

Songs of sadness and fear, of bravado and fore-shadowing, of wit and humor. Merry tunes to uplift the spirit and ease blistered feet. Songs of the South and songs of the North. Songs tinted blue and gray …

From simple homespun songs and folk melodies to the carefully crafted lyrics of polished poets and the music of skillful tunesmiths, from sources in the British Isles, the mountains of Tennessee and the rocky coast of Maine …

These then were the songs and tunes of the Civil War!

1861 to 1865

The Baritone Ukulele

★ The largest size ukulele, the baritone, is tuned DGBE with D being the lowest string and E the highest.

★ When the baritone accompanies the soprano, or plays the standard notation, the chord names will be the same for both instruments, but the chord shapes will be different. See the CHART OF MATCHING CHORDS for corresponding shapes.

★ The baritone can play the same tablature as the soprano, but it will sound four tones lower.

★ When the baritone plays the tablature, substitute the 2nd string 3rd fret for the open 4th string.

★ When the baritone plays the tablature, the chord shapes will be the same as those shown for the soprano, but they will have different names. See the CHART OF MATCHING CHORDS.

★ When the baritone plays the tablature and the soprano accompanies it, the soprano chords will have the same name but a different shape. See the CHART OF MATCHING CHORDS.

★ The baritone is tuned the same as the top four strings of the guitar. Therefore all the information related to the baritone also applies to the guitar.

IMPORTANT: If the baritone and soprano ukes play the same tablature, they will be in different keys. When the two are played together, let one uke play the standard notation or tablature and the other the accompanying chords.

Baritone

⭐ The Soprano Ukulele

★ The term "soprano" in this book refers to the three smallest ukes – the soprano, concert, and tenor – ranging in size upward from the smallest, the soprano. All three sizes are tuned the same to gCEA.

★ This is called standard or "C" tuning. Alternate tunings can be found on the Internet.

★ The small letter "g" indicates a higher pitch than the C and E in the familiar "My Dog Has Fleas" sequence. It has the same pitch as the 3rd fret of the 2nd string.

★ String numbers are: 4th string=g, 3rd string=C, 2nd string=E, and the 1st string=A.

★ All of the music in this collection has been scored for the soprano ukulele, as have the accompaniment chords and their letter names.

★ Because of the tuning and the range of the ukulele fingerboard, much of the following music is written in the key of B-flat. A frequently used chord in this key is the Eb, which is crowded and can be difficult for some players. Try substituting and Eb6 chord. It's easier to play by just barring all strings on the 3rd fret. See the MATCHING CHORD CHART for a diagram.

Soprano   *Concert*   *Tenor*

ALL QUIET ALONG THE POTOMAC TONIGHT

Ukulele tuning: gCEA

Words by
Ethel Lynn Beers

Music by
John Hill Hewitt

1.All qui-et a-long the Po - to-mac to-night, Ex - cept here and there a stray pick-et Is

shot as he walks on his beat to and fro, By a ri-fle-man hid in the thick-et. T'is

noth-ing, a pri-vate or two now and then, Will not count in the news of the bat-tle. Not an

ADDITIONAL LYRICS

2. All quiet along the Potomac tonight,
   Where the soldiers lie peacefully dreaming,
   And their tents in the rays of the clear autumn moon,
   And the light of the camp fires are gleaming;
   There's only the sound of the lone sentry's tread
   As he tramps from the rock to the fountain,
   And thinks of the two on the low trundle bed
   Far away in the cot on the mountain.

3. His musket falls slack, his face dark and grim
   Grows gentle with memories tender,
   As he mutters a prayer for the children asleep
   And their mother, "May heaven defend her!"
   The moon seems to shine as brightly as then,
   That night when the love yet unspoken,
   Leaped to his lips, and when low murmured vows
   Were pledged to be ever unbroken.

4. Then draws his sleeve roughly o'er his eyes,
   He dashes off the tears that are welling,
   And gathers his gun close up to his breast
   As if to keep down the heart's swelling.
   He passes the fountain, the blasted pine tree,
   And his footstep is lagging and weary,
   Yet onward he goes through the broad belt of light
   Toward the shades of the forest so dreary.

5. Hark! Was it the night wind that rustles the leaves!
   Was it the moonlight so wond'rously flashing?
   It looked like a rifle! "Ha, Mary, goodbye!"
   And his lifeblood is ebbing and splashing.
   All quiet along the Potomac tonight,
   No sound save the rush of the river;
   While soft falls the dew on the face of the dead,
   The picket's off duty for ever.

ANNIE LAURIE

*A Scottish song with lyrics from a poem written in the 1700s,
the tune from the early 1800s. It was well known to soldiers
on both sides, a fine song for singing that brought thoughts of
sweethearts and family members at home. Allegedly it was sung by
General Sherman's troops as they marched through Georgia while
torching the state and reducing much of it to smoldering ruins.*

Ukulele tuning: gCEA

Traditional

No small part of the song's charm are the octave leaps of melody, soaring from low C to high C. You'll see them in the 1st full measure, in the 5th, and in the next to last measure. In tablature those jumps are from the open 3rd string to the 3rd fret of the 1st string.

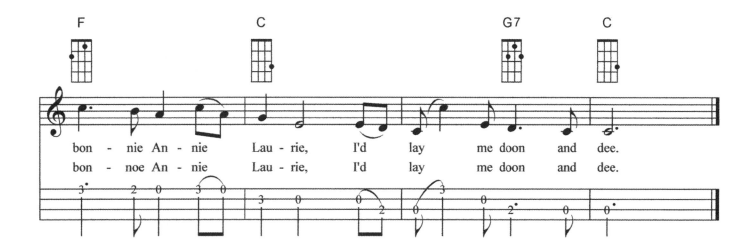

ADDITIONAL LYRICS

3. Like dew on the gowan lying
   Is the fa' o' her fairy feet,
   And like winds in summer sighing,
   Her voice is low and sweet;
   Her voice is low and sweet,
   And she's a' the world to me,
   And for bonnie Annie Laurie,
   I'd lay me doon and dee.

"My plans are perfect, and when I start to carry them out, may God have mercy on Bobby Lee, for I shall have none."

General 'Fighting' Joe Hooker

AURA LEA

Ukulele tuning: gCEA

Words by:
George R. Poulton

Music by:
W.W. Fosdick

2. In thy blush the rose was born, music when you spake.
   Through thine azure eye the morn, sparkling seemed to break.
   Aura Lea, Aura Lea, birds of crimson wing
   Never song have sung to me as in that night, sweet spring.

3. Aura Lea, the bird may flee the willow's golden hair,
   Swing through winter fitfully on the stormy air.
   Yet if thy blue eyes I see, gloom will soon depart.
   For to me sweet Aura Lea is sunshine through the heart.

4. When the mistletoe was green, midst the winter's snows,
   Sunshine in thy face was seen kissing lips of rose.
   Aura Lea, Aura Lea, take my golden ring;
   Love and light return with thee, and swallows with the spring.

Men of the famous "Vermont Brigade" all from the one state, which suffered more heavily than any other federal brigade during the war. Within a week at the wilderness and Spotsylvania, it lost 1,645 out of 2,100 men.

THE BATTLE CRY OF FREEDOM

Ukulele tuning: gCEA

Words & Music
GEORGE F. ROOT

ADDITIONAL LYRICS

2. We are springing to the call
   For three hundred thousand more,
   Shouting the battle cry of freedom,
   And we'll fill the vacant ranks
   Of our brothers gone before,
   Shouting the battle cry of freedom!
   CHORUS

3. We will welcome to our numbers
   The loyal true and brave,
   Shouting the battle cry of freedom,
   And altho' he may be poor
   He shall never be a slave,
   Shouting the battle cry of freedom!
   CHORUS

4. So we're springing to the call!
   From the East and from the West,
   Shouting the battle cry of freedom,
   And we'll hurl the rebel crew
   From the land that we love best,
   Shouting the battle cry of freedom!
   CHORUS

BATTLE HYMN of the REPUBLIC

Ukulele tuning: gCEA

Words by
JULIA WARD HOWE

Music by
WILLIAM STEFFE

The melody of this song is the same as the one for JOHN BROWN'S BODY. The tune was written shortly before the the Civil War with lyrics added to become the spiritual CANAAN'S HAPPY SHORE. With a change of lyrics in 1861, the song evolved into JOHN BROWN'S BODY. Julia Ward Howe, a supporter of the Union and the anti-slavery movement, heard the song at a military review and was inspired to write new words to the tune. The marriage of her lyrics with the popular tune has resulted in one of the best known examples of American patriotic music.

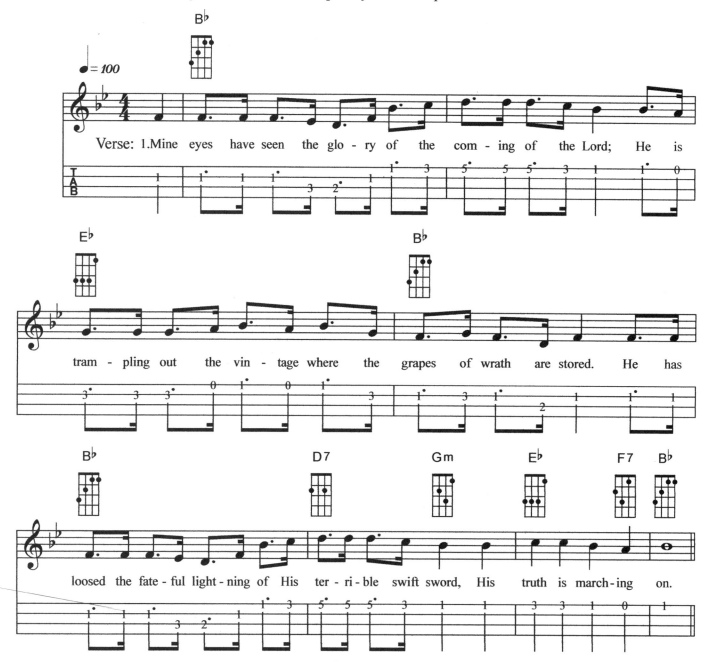

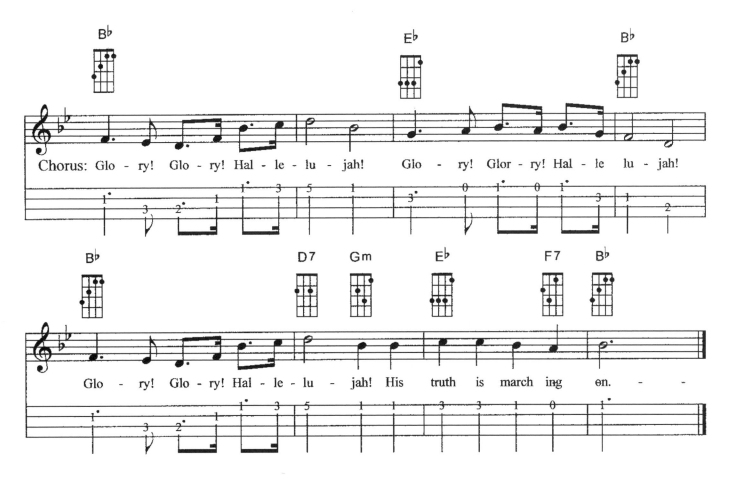

ADDITIONAL VERSES

2. I have seen Him in the watch-fires of a hundred circling camps,
   They have builded Him an altar in the evening dews and damps;
   I can read His righteous sentence by the dim and flaring lamps:
   His day is marching on.
   CHORUS

3. I have read a fiery gospel writ in burnished rows of steel:
   "As ye deal with my contemners, so with you My grace shall deal;
   Let the Hero, born of woman, crush the serpent with His heel,
   Since God is marching on."
   CHORUS

4. He has sounded forth the trumpet that shall never call retreat;
   He is sifting out the hearts of men before His judgment seat:
   Oh, be swift, my soul, to answer Him! be jubilant, my feet!
   Our God is marching on.
   CHORUS

5. In the beauty of the lillies Christ has born across the sea,
   With a glory in His bosom that tansfigures you and me:
   As He died to make men holy, let us die to make men free,
   While God is marching on.
   CHORUS

THE BONNIE BLUE FLAG

Ukulele tuning: gCEA

HARRY MACARTHUR

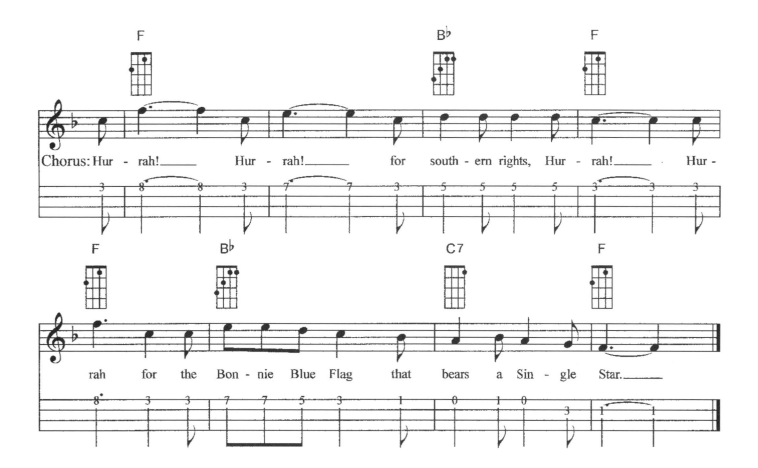

Chorus: Hur - rah!_____ Hur - rah!_____ for south - ern rights, Hur - rah!_____ · Hur - rah for the Bon - nie Blue Flag that bears a Sin - gle Star._____

ADDITIONAL LYRICS

2. As long as the Union was faithful to her trust,
   Like friends and like bretheren kind were we and just;
   But now when Northern treachery attempts our rights to mar,
   We hoist on high the Bonnie Blue Flag that bears a Single Star.
   CHORUS

3. First, gallant South Carolina nobly made the stand;
   Then came Alabama, who took her by the hand;
   Next, quickly Mississippi, Georgia and Florida;
   All raised on high the Bonnie Blue Flag that bears a Single Star.
   CHORUS

4. Ye men of valor, gather round the Banner of the Right,
   Texas and fair Louisiana, join us in the fight;
   Davis, our loved president, and Stephens, Stateman rare,
   Now rally round the Bonnie Blue Flag that bears a Single Star.
   CHORUS

5. And here's to brave Virginia! The Old Dominion State
   With the young Confederacy at length has linked her fate;
   Impelled by her example, now other States prepare
   To hoist on high the Bonnie Blue Flag that bears a Single Star.
   CHORUS

6. Then cheer, boys, raise the joyous shout,
   For Arkansas and North Carolina now have both gone out;
   And let another rousing cheer for Tennessee be given,
   The Single Star of the Bonnie Blue Flag has grown to be eleven.
   CHORUS

7. Then here's to our Confederacy, strong we are and brave,
   Like patriots of old, we'll fight our heritage to save;
   And rather than submit to shame, to die we would prefer,
   So cheer for the Bonnie Blue Flag that bear a Single Star.
   CHORUS

8. FINAL CHORUS:
   Hurrah! Hurrah! for Southern Rights, hurrah!
   Hurrah! for the Bonnie Blue Flag has gained th'Eleventh Star.

DIXIE

Ukulele tuning: gCEA

DANIEL D. EMMETT

Dan Emmett, a blackface minstrel performer and banjoist, was a northener who begrudged the South having adopted his song. But even President Lincoln admitted it was one of his favorites. The song is more memorable for its tune and the lyric given here than for alternative lyrics in black dialect, which unlike "old times there" have mostly been forgotten.

General Ulysses S. Grant signed *Carte de Visite.*

A Robert E. Lee singed *Carte de Visite,* (calling card) taken in 1863 by Julian Vannerson of Richmond, Virginia, one of the most famous wartime portraits of General Lee.

GARRYOWEN

An Irish "quickstep" that was a favorite of General Custer's 7th Cavalry Regiment. Custer liked the tune's cadence which he felt was particularly good for marching horses. Even before the Civil War it was the official marching tune of New York's "Fighting 69th" Infantry Regiment. Supposedly it was the last tune played before"Custer's Last Stand" at the Battle of Little Bighorn.

Ukulele tuning: gCEA

Traditional

THE GIRL I LEFT BEHIND ME

Ukulele tuning: gCEA

TRADITIONAL

1.I am lone - some since I crossed the hill and o'er the moor and

val - ley, such heav - ey thoughts my heart do fill since part - ing with my Sal - ly. I

seek no more the fine and gay, for each but doth re - mind me how swift the hours did

pass a - way with the girl I left be - hind me.

24

With roots in Ireland and England that trace back to the late 1700s and early 1800s, the lyrics and melody of this song have since undergone innumerable variations. Civil War troops marched to it with banners flying and the spirited sound of flute and drums. It was well known as an Army marching song in the War of 1812. Confederate troops lampooned the song's last eight measures with "Jeff Davis is a gentleman, Abe Lincoln is a fool. Jeff Davis rides a big white horse, Abe Lincoln rides a mule." Appropriately, the tune is played at West Point graduations to march cadets off to their new assignments.

ADDITIONAL LYRICS

2. Her golden hair, her ringlets fair,
   Her eyes like shining diamonds,
   Her slender waist, her heavenly face,
   That leaves my heart still pining.
   Ye gods above, O hear my prayer,
   Kind heaven, may favor find me,
   And send me safely back again
   To the girl I left behind me.

3. My mind her form shall still retain,
   In sleeping or in waking,
   Until I see my love again
   For whom my heart is breaking.
   If ever I should see the day
   When Mars shall have resigned me,
   For evermore I'll glady stay
   With the girl I left behind me.

4. The bee shall honey taste no more,
   The dove become a ranger,
   The dashing waves shall cease to roar,
   Ere she's to me a stranger.
   The vows we registered above
   Shall ever cheer and binbd me,
   In constancy to her I love,
   The girl I left behind me,

"War is cruelty. There is no use trying to reform it. The crueler it is, the sooner it will be over."

General William Tecumseh Sherman

GOOBER PEAS

A fabled staple of the Confederate diet -- boiled peanuts!

Ukulele tuning: gCEA

Traditional

Verse: 1.Sit-ting by the road-side on a sum-mer's day, chat-ting with my mess-mates, pass-ing time a-way,

ly-ing in the shad-ow un-der-neath the trees. Good-ness how de-li-cious, eat-ing goo-ber peas.

Chorus: Peas, peas, peas, peas, eat-ing goo-ber peas. Good-ness, how de-li-cious, eat-ing goo-ber peas.

ADDITIONAL VERSES

2. When a horseman passes, the soldiers have a rule
   To cry out at their loudest, "Mister, here's your mule!"
   But still another pleasure enchanting-er than these
   Is wearing out your grinders, eating goober peas!
   CHORUS

3. Just before the battle, the Gen'ral hears a row,
   He says, "The Yanks are coming, I hear their rifles now!"
   He turns around in wonder, and what do you think he sees?
   The Georgia Militia, eating goober peas!
   CHORUS

4. I think my song has lasted almost long enough,
   The subject's interesting, the rhymes are mighty rough.
   I wish this war was over, free from rags and fleas,
   We'd kiss our wives and sweethearts, and gobble goober peas!
   CHORUS

"Jackson possessed the brutality essential in war; Lee did not. He could clasp the hand of a wounded enemy, whilst Jackson ground his teeth and murmured, 'No quarter to the violators of our homes and firesides', and when someone deplored the necessity of destroying so many brave men, he exclaimed: 'No, shoot them all, I do not wish them to be brave.'"

Major General J.F.C. Fuller, *British military writer, on Stonewall Jackson*

HOME, SWEET HOME

Ukulele tuning: gCEA

Words by
JOHN HOWARD PAYNE

Music by
HENRY R. BISHOP

In all probability, this was the most beloved song of both Federal and Confederate soldiers. Regimental bands played it before, during, and after battles, often within earshot of each other, sometimes with both sides playing it together in something of a "battle of the bands." At evening's close when campfires were lit and patriotic tunes concluded, HOME, SWEET HOME brought the soldiers a calming sense of peace and purpose as to what they were fighting for. The song is said to have been a favorite of Abraham Lincoln and was performed for him in the White House at his own request.

1.Mid pleas - ures and pal - a - ces though we may roam, Be it
2.An ex - ile from home, splend - or daz - zles in vain. Oh!

ev - er so hum - ble, There's no place like home. A
give me my low - ly thatched cot - tage a - gain! The

charm from the skies seems to hal - low us there, Which
birds sing - ing gai - ly that came at my call; Give me

ADDITIONAL LYRICS

3. I gaze at the moon as I tread the drear wild,
   And feel that my mother now thinks of her child;
   As she looks on that moon from our own cottage door,
   Thro' the woodbine whose fragrance shall cheer me no more.
         Home, home, sweet, sweet home,
         There's no place like home,
         There's no place like home.

JOHN BROWN'S BODY

Ukulele tuning: gCEA

Traditional

John Brown was a Northern abolitionist who advocated violent oppostion to slavery. In 1859 he led a raid on the Federal armory at Harpers Ferry, West Virginia, in a failed attempt to gain weapons for a slave rebellion. Brown was captured, tried for treason, and executed. The raid is considered to have been a major factor in the start of the Civil War. The song was popular with marching Union troops.

ADDITIONAL VERSES

2. He captured Harpers Ferry with his nineteen men so true,
   He frightened old Virginia 'til she trembled through and through.
   They hanged him for a traitor, themselves the traitor's crew,
   His soul goes marching on. CHORUS

3. He's gone to be a soldier in the army of the Lord (3 times),
   His soul goes marching on. CHORUS

4. The stars above in heaven are a-lookin' kindly down (3 times),
   His soul goes marching on. CHORUS

5. We'll hang Jeff Davis from a sour apple tree (3 times),
   As we go marching on. CHORUS

JUST BEFORE THE BATTLE, MOTHER

Ukulele tuning: gCEA

Words & Music
GEORGE F. ROOT

ADDITIONAL VERSES

2. O, I long to see you, Mother,
   And the loving ones at home;
   But, I'll never leave our banner,
   Till in honor I can come.
   Tell the traitors all around you,
   That their cruel words we know
   In ev'ry battle kill our soldiers
   By the help they give the foe.
   CHORUS

3. Hark! I hear the bugles sounding,
   T'is the signal for the fight.
   Now may God protect us, Mother,
   As He ever does the right.
   Hear the "Battle Cry of Freedom,"
   How it swells upon the air;
   Oh yes, we'll rally round the standard,
   Or we'll perish nobly there.
   CHORUS

KATHLEEN MAVOURNEEN

Ukulele tuning: gCEA

Words by
MARION CRAWFORD

Music by
FREDERICK CROUCH

The first time I heard this touchingly sentimental song it was sung by Irish tenor John McCormack and, frankly, it brought tears to my eyes. It was somewhat similar for Confederate General Lewis A. Armistead as reported in Michael Shaara's book about the Battle of Gettysburg, THE KILLER ANGELS, and Bruce Catton's THE CIVIL WAR. Armistead was attending a dinner party hosted by his close friend, future Union General Winfield Scott Hancock. As one of the guests sang the song while accompanying herself on the piano, tears welled up in Armistead's eyes. The words of parting seemed especially appropriate since many of the guests would be separated by allegiance to different sides in the ensuing war -- Armistead to the Southern cause, Hancock to the Northern. How prophetic the lyrics, "It may be for years and it may be forever." The two generals, despite their strong bond of friendship, reluctantly faced each other at Gettysburg. Armistead was killed. Hancock, though severely wounded, survived.

1.Kath - leen Ma - vour - neen! The gray dawn is break - ing, The horn of the
2.Kath - leen Ma - vour - neen! A - wake from thy slum - bers, The blue moun - tains

hunt - er____ is heard on the hill, The lark from her light wing the
glow in____ the sun's gold - en light, Ah! where is the spell that once

bright dew is shak - ing, Kath - leen____ Ma - vour - neen! What slum - bring still? Oh!
hung on thy num - bers, A - rise in____ thy beau - ty thou star of my night! Ma -

KINGDOM COMING

Ukulele tuning: gCEA

HENRY C. WORK

Verse: 1.Say, dar-keys, hab you seen de mas-sa wid de muff-stash on his face? Go

long de road some time dis morn-in' like he gwine to leab de place. He

seen a smoke, way up de rib-ber, whar de Link-um gum-boats lay; he

took his hat an' lef ber-ry sud-den, an' I spec he's run a-way!

The composer, Henry Clay Work, wrote other well known songs including "Marching Through Georgia" and "My Grandfather's Clock," the latter having given rise to calling tall standing clocks by that name. His song "The Ship That Never Returned" was parodied in 1959 by the folk group Kingston Trio as "The M.T.A. Song" (also known as "Charlie On The M.T.A."). The melody has further been adapted for the song "Wreck Of The Old '97."

ADDITIONAL VERSES

2. He six foot one way, two foot tudder, an' he weigh tree hundred pound,
   His coat so big he couldn't pay de tailor, an' it won't go half way round.
   He drill so much dey call him Cap'an, an' he get so drefful tann'd,
   I spec he try an' fool dem Yankees for to tink he's contraband.
   CHORUS

3. De darkeys feel so lonesome libbing in de log house on de lawn,
   Dey move dar tings to massa's parlor for to keep it while he's gone.
   Dar's wine an' cider in de kitchen, an' de darkeys dey'll hab some,
   I spose dey'll all be cornfiscated when de Linkum sojers come.
   CHORUS

4. De oberseer he make us trouble, an' he dribe us round a spell,
   We lock him up in de smokehouse cellar, wid de key trown in de well.
   De whip is lost, de han'cuff broken, but de massa'll hab his pay,
   He's ole enough, big enough, ought to known better dan to went an' run away.
   CHORUS

LORENA

Joseph P. Webster Ukulele tuning: gCEA **Rev. H. D. L. Webster**

"Lorena" was immensely popular with both Union and Confederate soldiers for whom it brought longing and heartaches for loved ones at home. The lyrics, written by a northern minister, sadly reflect the breakup of his relationship with a sweetheart whose family objected to him as an unsuitable suitor. The words were set to music written by the composer of the spiritual "In The Sweet By And By". The song was published in 1858 just prior to the start of the Civil War.

ADDITIONAL LYRICS

2. A hundred months have passed, Lorena,
   Since last I held that hand in mine,
   And felt the pulse beat fast, Lorena,
   Though mine beat faster far than thine.
   A hundred months, 'twas flowery May,
   When up the hilly slope we climbed,
   To watch the dying of the day,
   And hear the distant church bells chime.

3. We loved each other then, Lorena,
   More than we ever dared to tell;
   And what might have been, Lorena,
   Had but our lovings prospered well.
   But then 'tis past, the years are gone,
   I'll not call up their shadowy forms;
   I'll say to them, "Lost years, sleep on!
   Sleep on! nor heed life's pelting storms."

4. Yes, these were words of mine, Lorena,
   They burn within my memory yet;
   They touched some tender chords, Lorena,
   Which thrill and tremble with regret.
   'Twas not thy woman's heart that spoke;
   Thy heart was always true to me.
   A duty, stern and passing, broke
   The tie which linked my soul with thee.

"We'll fight them, sir, 'til hell freezes over, and then, sir, we will fight them on the ice."

A Confederate soldier at Gettysburg, in *The Civil War by Shelby Foote*

MARCHING THROUGH GEORGIA

Ukulele tuning: gCEA

Words and music
HENRY CLAY WORK

MARYLAND, MY MARYLAND

Ukulele tuning: gCEA

Traditional

Maryland was a borderline state between the North and the South, with strong allegiances to both sides, and is sometimes referred to as a "house divided." Although it was a slave state, it aligned with the North despite many of its citizens joining the Rebel cause. The song, which supports the Southern cause, became a battle anthem for the Confederacy and urges Maryland to take up arms and fight the Union. The familiar melody is the same as the German Christmas carol, O TANNENBAUM. It has also been adopted by universities and fraternities, as well as for state songs besides that of Maryland.

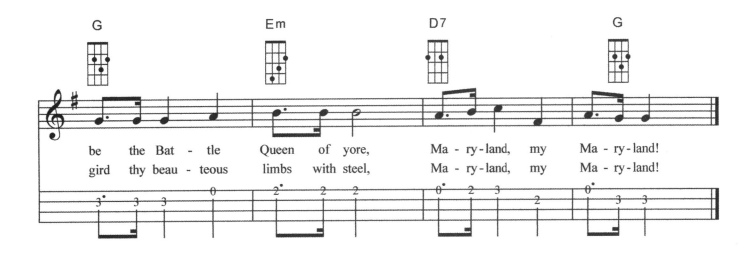

| G | Em | D7 | G |

be   the Bat - tle   Queen   of yore,   Ma - ry - land,   my   Ma - ry - land!
gird   thy beau - teous   limbs   with steel,   Ma - ry - land,   my   Ma - ry - land!

ADDITIONAL LYRICS

3. Come! for thy shield is bright and strong,
Maryland! My Maryland!
Come! for thy dalliance does thee wrong,
Maryland! My Maryland!
Come! to thine own heroic throng
That stalks with Liberty along,
And gives a new key to the song,
Maryland! My Maryland!

4. I hear the distant thunder-hum,
Maryland! My Maryland!
The Old Line's bugle, fife and drum,
Maryland! My Maryland!
She is not dead, nor deaf, nor dumb --
Huzza! she spurns the Northern scum!
She breathes -- she burns! she'll come! She'll come!
Maryland! My Maryland.

"It is well that war is so terrible, else we should grow too fond of it."

General Lee to General Longstreet

General James Ewell Brown (JEB) Stuart was the most famous, daring and flamboyant cavalry commander in the Civil War.

A Civil War recruiting broadside for the 34th N.Y. Regiment. The poster goes on to list the pay, clothing allowance, rations, bounty of $100, and even promises 160 acres of land to each recruit to sign up. Unfortunately, there is no record of the regimental company ever fulfilling its ranks.

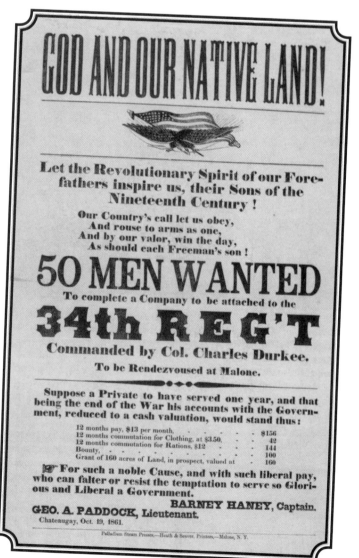

OH, SHENANDOAH

*Originally a work song for hoisting anchor and sails, this sea chanty reached dry land,
and like many folk songs, eventually acquired a number of lyric variations. The name
"Shenandoah" appealed to soldiers who may have associated it with a home west of the
Missouri River in Shenandoah, Iowa, or one in the Shenandoah Valley, or nearby the
Shenandoah River that joined the Potomac River at Harpers Ferry, site of John Brown's raid.*

Ukulele tuning: gCEA

Traditional

SHENANDOAH -- the rich, fertile Valley of Virginia, the so-called
granary and bread basket of the Confederate army. In a Federal
scorched-earth policy, the Valley was devastated by the Army of the
Shenandoah under the command of General "Little Phil" Sheridan.
Although small in stature, measuring just five foot four inches, a
foot shorter than Abraham Lincoln, Sheridan was a fierce warrior
and brilliant commander, a favorite of General Ulysses S. Grant.

TENTING ON THE OLD CAMP GROUND

Ukulele tuning: gCEA

Words & Music
WALTER KITTREDGE

Verse: 1. We're tent-ing to-night on the old camp ground, give us a song to cheer, our

wear - y hearts a song of home and friends we love so dear.

Chorus: Man-y are the hearts that are wear-y to-night, wish-ing for the war to cease;

Many are the hearts look-ing for the right to see the dawn of peace.

Tent-ing to-night, tent-ing to-night tent-ing on the old camp ground.
*Dy-ing on the old camp ground.

* 4th verse CHORUS.

ADDITIONAL VERSES

2. We've been tenting tonight on the old camp ground,
   Thinking of days gone by,
   Of the loved ones at home that gave us the hand,
   And tear that said "Goodbye."
   CHORUS

3. We are tired of war on the old camp ground,
   Many are dead and gone,
   Of the brave and true who've left their homes,
   Others been wounded long.
   CHORUS

4. We've been fighting today on the old camp ground,
   Many are lying near;
   Some are dead and some are dying,
   Many are in tears.
   CHORUS

TRAMP! TRAMP! TRAMP!

Words & Music
GE0RGE F. ROOT

Ukulele tuning: gCEA

Despite the lively lilt of the melody, the song reflects defeat, capture, and the subsequent hard life of a prison camp. Conditions were deplorable. Death, disease, and depression were rampant. But one soldier attempts to bring hope and to uplift the morale of his fellow prisioners. Help is on the way. Liberation will soon come. Peace and restoration to family and friends are not far off.

Chorus: Tramp, tramp, tramp, the boys are march-ing, cheer up, com-rades, they will come. And be-neath the star-ry flag, we shall breathe the air a-gain of our free-land in our own be-lov-ed home.

ADDITIONAL VERSES

2. In the battle front we stood when their fiercest charge they made,
   And they swept us off a hundred men or more,
   But before we reached their lines, they were beaten back dismayed,
   And we heard the cry of vict'ry o'er and o'er. CHORUS

3. So within the prison cell, we are waiting for the day
   That will come to open wide the iron door,
   And the hollow eye grows bright, and the poor heart almost gay,
   As we think of seeing home and friends once more. CHORUS

WE ARE COMING, FATHER ABRA'AM

Ukulele tuning: gCEA

Words by
J. S. Gibbons

Music by
L.O. Emerson

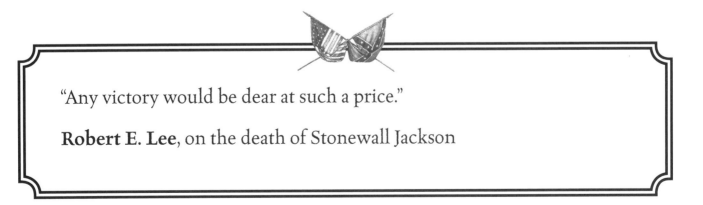

"Any victory would be dear at such a price."

Robert E. Lee, on the death of Stonewall Jackson

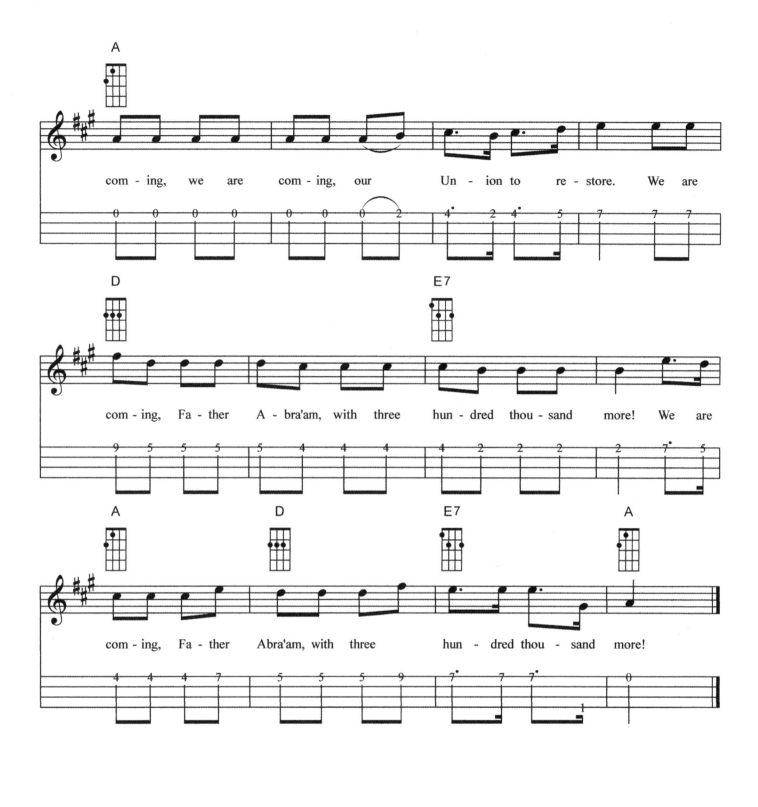

com - ing, we are com - ing, our Un - ion to re - store. We are

com - ing, Fa - ther A - bra'am, with three hun - dred thou - sand more! We are

com - ing, Fa - ther Abra'am, with three hun - dred thou - sand more!

"A rich man's war and a poor man's fight..."

Southern opposition slogan, in *The Civil War by Shelby Foote*

President Lincoln put out a call in 1862 for 300,000 volunteers to fill the ranks of the Union army depleted by a number of Northern losses. The song was in a sense a response to that call. The lyrics were originally a poem that appeared in a New York newspaper, later set to music by several composers, including Stephen Foster. Attribution of both lyrics and music, however, is questionable. The ones listed here seem to be the most creditable.

ADDITIONAL VERSES

2. If you look across the hilltops that meet the northern sky,
   Long moving lines of rising dust your vision may descry;
   And now the wind, an instant, tears the cloudy veil aside,
   And floats aloft our spangled flag in glory and in pride;
   And bayonets in the sunlight gleam, and bands brave music pour,
   We are coming, Father Abra'am, three hundred thousand more!
   CHORUS:
       We are coming, we are coming, our Union to restore;
       We are coming, Father Abra'am, with three hundred thousand more,
       We are coming, Father Abra'am, with three hundred thousand more!

3. If you look up all our valleys where growing harvests shine,
   You may see our sturdy farmer boys fast forming into line;
   And children from their mother's knees are pulling at the weeds,
   And learning how to reap and sow against their country's needs;
   And a farewell group stands weeping at every cottage door,
   We are coming, Father Abra'am, three hundred thousand more!
   CHORUS

4. You have called us, and we're coming, by Richmond's bloody tide,
   To lay us down for freedom's sake, our brothers' bones beside;
   Or from foul treason's savage group, to wrench the murderous blade,
   And in the face of foreign foes its fragments to parade;
   Six hundred thousand loyal men and true have gone before,
   We are coming, Father Abra'am, three hundred thousand more!
   CHORUS

"If I tap that little bell, I can send you to a place where you will never hear the dogs bark."

United States Secretary of War **Stanton**

WEEPING, SAD AND LONELY

Ukulele tuning: gCEA

Words by
CHARLES CARROLL SAWYER

Music by
HENRY TUCKER

Verse: 1.Dear - est love, do you re - mem - ber when we last did meet,

how you told me that you loved me, kneel - ing at my feet?

Oh! how proud you stood be - fore me, in your suit of blue,

ADDITIONAL VERSES

2. When the summer breeze is sighing,
Mournfuly, along!
Or when autumn leaves are falling,
Sadly breathes the song.
Oft in dreams I see thee lying
On the battle plain,
Lonely, wounded, even dying,
Calling out in vain.
CHORUS

3. If amid the din of battle,
Nobly you should fall,
Far away from those who love you,
None to hear you call.
Who would whisper words of comfort,
Who would soothe your pain?
Ah! the many cruel fancies
Ever in my brain.
CHORUS

4. But our country called you, darling,
Angels cheer your way,
While our nation's sons are fighting,
We can only pray.
Nobly strike for God and liberty,
Let all nations see
How we love our starry banner,
Emblem of the free.
CHORUS

55

WHEN JOHNNY COMES MARCHING HOME

Ukulele tuning: gCEA

LOUIS LAMBERT

2. The old church bell will peel with joy,
   Hurrah! Hurrah!
   To welcome home our darling boy,
   Hurrah! Hurrah!
   The village lads and lassies say,
   With roses they will strew the way,
   And we'll all feel gay,
   When Jonny comes marching home.

3. Get ready for the jubilee,
   Hurrah! Hurrah!
   We'll give the hero three times three,
   Hurrah! Hurrah!
   The laurel wreath is ready now,
   To place upon his loyal brow,
   And we'll all feel gay,
   When Johnny comes marching home.

4. Let love and friendship on that day,
   Hurrah! Hurrah!
   Their choices treasures then display,
   Hurrah! Hurrah!
   And let each one perform some part,
   To fill with joy the warrior's heart,
   And we'll all feel gay,
   When Johnny comes marching home.

"Jackson possessed the brutality essential in war; Lee did not. He could clasp the hand of a wounded enemy, whilst Jackson ground his teeth and murmured, 'No quarter to the violators of our homes and firesides', and when someone deplored the necessity of destroying so many brave men, he exclaimed: 'No, shoot them all, I do not wish them to be brave.'"

Major General J.F.C. Fuller, British military writer, on Stonewall Jackson

THE YELLOW ROSE OF TEXAS

Ukulele tuning: gCEA

Traditional

2. She's the sweetest rose of color this soldier ever knew,
   Her eyes as bright as diamonds, they sparkle like the dew;
   You may talk about your dearest May, and sing of Rosa Lee,
   But the yellow rose of Texas beats the belles of Tennessee.

3. When the Rio Grande is flowing and the starry skies are bright,
   She walks along the river in the quiet summer night;
   I think that she remembers, when we parted long ago,
   I promised to come back again and not to leave her so.

4. Oh, now I'm going to find her for my heart is full of woe,
   And we'll sing the songs together that we sung so long ago;
   We'll play the banjo gaily, and we'll sing the songs of yore,
   And the yellow rose of Texas shall be mine forevermore.

5. Oh, my feet are torn and bloody, and my heart is full of woe,
   I'm going back to Georgia to find my Uncle Joe,
   You may talk about your Beauregard and sing of General Lee,
   But the gallant Hood of Texas played hell in Tennessee.*

*Names refer to Confederate generals: Joseph Johnson, P.G.T. Beauregard,
   Robert E. Lee, and John Bell Hood.

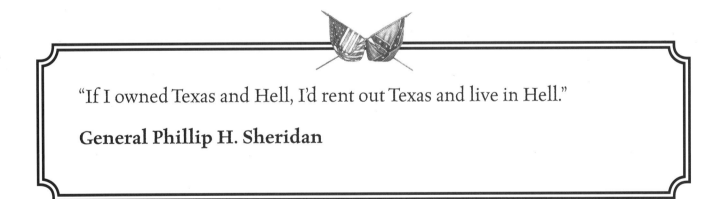

"If I owned Texas and Hell, I'd rent out Texas and live in Hell."

General Phillip H. Sheridan

CHART OF MATCHING CHORDS

*These are the shapes of chords for the songs and tunes
included in this book.*